TIME TO GET INTO POSITION

Charleston, SC
www.PalmettoPublishing.com

Time to Get Into Position
Copyright © 2021 by Stasha Starr

All rights reserved
No portion of this book may be reproduced, stored in a retrieval system, or transmitted in any form by any means–electronic, mechanical, photocopy, recording, or other–except for brief quotations in printed reviews, without prior permission of the author.

First Edition

Paperback ISBN: 978-1-68515-048-8
eBook ISBN: 978-1-68515-049-5

TIME TO GET INTO POSITION

Stasha Starr

This book is dedicated to the following:
First and foremost, my children: Kamiyah, Mario and Majesty.
Everything I do in this life is for you and your future.

To Amber, you definitely got the keys.

And to Nancy Phon, always remember to
keep your head above your shoulders, sis.

INTRODUCTION

THE NUMBER 75669-097 SHALL FOREVER BE EMBEDDED in my brain, *never* to be forgotten. Indicted on April 20, 2016, that was the number assigned to me when I was sentenced to fifty months in federal prison. Even before I heard the deafening crash of those steel, cell doors slamming behind me, the only thought that continually played over and over in my mind, like a CD on repeat, was what was I going to do to not end up back in that hellhole. But, I wasn't just interested in returning to my life; I needed to leave this horrible experience much better than how I came into this situation; for my children's sake, if for no other reason. My daughter had just gone into remission from cancer, and I had delivered my newborn baby boy on my fifth day in custody. More than ever, they were my focus, my lifeline. The pain of not being with my beautiful children, especially during their most formative stages of life, still haunts me to this day. But I knew that I just needed to remain uplifted during this troubling time so that when I did return to them, they would not see any of the old me or experience any of my past brokenness.

During this time, I realized that poverty isn't only the state of being extremely poor; it can also speak to your mindset. Shortly after starting my jail term, I realized that I had been living in a state of mental poverty. I was broken. Most women incarcerated in federal prisons are there, mostly because of drug-related offenses, extortion, fraud or bribery. One of the things we all, too often, had in common, and was the reason that landed us in our unfortunate predicaments, was that we were all trying to get to that "bag." All we knew was that we wanted it very badly, and too often, we were willing to do just about anything to get it; by any means necessary. But exactly how could we secure the "bag" legally?

Another common denominator among us (which seemed like an even greater problem to me), was that nearly 80 percent of us lacked any financial literacy or knowledge, in how to go about doing it legally. A large percentage of us did not come from wealthy families. Some of the many things they don't teach you in the public school system are how to build credit, start a business, make "good" money, or just create and maintain financial wealth—and eventually, generational wealth! And since I couldn't find a program, tutorial or book to teach women this important information about starting a new, financially sound life after prison, I am here to give you the steps I took to get me where I'm at today. It hasn't been an easy road by any means, but ten months before I was to be released from prison, my mindset really started to shift. I knew that after my release, I'd have to be in total control of my life going forward: physically, spiritually and yes, financially. This, of course, meant that it was ***Time to Get Into Position***.

CONTENTS

Introduction VII

Chapter One 1
MONEY IS JUST A TOOL

Chapter Two 11
MONEY MANAGEMENT

Chapter Three 19
CHECK MY CREDIT; MY
NAME'S GOOD

Chapter Four 35
ROME WASN'T BUILT IN A DAY

Chapter Five 41
LEVERAGE MORE THAN WHAT'S
BETWEEN YOUR LEGS

Chapter One

MONEY IS JUST A TOOL

A MERE 5 PERCENT OF THE WORLD'S POPULATION ENJOYS generational wealth. The middle class makes up 15 percent and the working class 80 percent. It's very important that you fully understand the difference between these terms.

Generational (or asset) wealth refers to assets passed down from one generation of a family to the next. Assets often include stocks, bonds, real estate, and, more than likely, a family business. As a parent, can you imagine being financially savvy enough to take your money and wisely invest it so that your kids won't have to worry about the security of their futures? College tuitions will be covered, as will down payments for their first homes. As a matter of fact, if assets are managed properly, even their descendants will be set for life. I remember my first time reading about generational wealth and, of course, I immediately thought of my children.

What could I possibly do to achieve and maintain this kind of wealth for them? At the time, I had my eight-year-old daughter, my three-year-old son, and a baby boy, whom I had delivered just five days into my incarceration, and was allowed to hold for only a brief moment before he was taken away from me.

To say that my children were on my mind daily would be the understatement of the century. And not just because I was physically separated from them; unable to hold, hug and kiss them. I knew that once I was released, my primary goal, (other than not ending back up in prison), was to reclaim my life and to ensure a better future for all of us…my babies and me. So how was I going to do this? When you think about generational wealth, you have to think about some of the richest families in the world: the Rockefellers (Oil), the Waltons (Walmart), and even the Trumps (real estate). These families have made so much money over the decades, that even if they never earn another penny, their financial futures are secure. But, of course, having generational/asset wealth passed down to you isn't enough. Earning an education, and learning, how to maintain and grow this money is more important than just having it handed to you. See anybody can get rich, but staying rich involves having a totally different mindset. Making money is an action, keeping it is a behavior and growing it—well, that takes knowledge! That's why it's so important to understand the value of money. By knowing that it's more than just paper currency to be exchanged for goods, you must be educated and you should strategize to make your money work for you and your family.

Below the generational-wealth class of people, there is the middle class. "Middle Class" is, as it suggests, the description given to individuals and households who fall between the upper class (generational wealth) and the working class. One major difference between the middle and working classes is often a college education. Those who fall into the middle class range are often employed as managers and civil servants at companies that offer retirement and 401(K) plans. Hey there's nothing wrong with these types of jobs, but once I became aware of the term "generational wealth," there was no turning back for me…I was sold! I didn't get into this position in federal prison by living paycheck to paycheck. Believe it or not, even in these circumstances I still consider myself a young boss—yep, humble as ever in my brown khakis, but my confidence is not broken at all, and my vision is fixed.

See whether you sold dope, were a scammer or ran an illegal enterprise, believe it or not, you had already positioned yourself as a boss running a business! You were already dealing with money in exchange for goods, which resulted in a profit. Sadly, though, you probably mismanaged your money and and did not understand its value. More importantly, it may have not been the right business to create generational wealth, but more than likely, it created generational curses, unknowingly, setting your kids up for the same failures and traps that, too often, our parents had set for us. Lord knows, it was better to have been in prison than to have ended up in a morgue, but I was determined to change my environment and my "poor man's" mindset, and, once released, make my life and time count.

The bottom rung on society's ladder of life is the working class, with many not even living above the poverty line. Poverty is a state or condition in which a person in our community lacks the financial resources essential for a minimum standard of living. You are often just operating off survival mode with government programs like welfare, food stamps, and Section 8 housing. Trust me when I tell you that I speak of this life from experience—hood living from day to day. I would sometimes think about all the times I had to go into survival mode just to make it through to the that day, living a life with no real plan for a real future, just constantly out there trying to hustle and make some fast money (often just enough money to make it to the next day—or make it through *that* day, for that matter).

I remember as a kid not being able to go and hang out over at my friend's house because they too were in survival mode, and like us, they were not sure where their next meal would be coming from. This pervasive attitude usually stems from the lack of resources and education. It's a world where the blind is too often leading the blind. Instead of wealth and knowledge, bad information is being passed down from generation to generation, setting into play generational curses. When I was out doing what I was doing (mostly scamming), I never really thought much about it and definitely did not view it as something that wrong because my entire family was either doing the same thing at that time or had done it in the past. Generational curses. The game had been passed right down to me and my only objective was to do it bigger and better than anyone in my family...and not get caught.

But how does one go from day-to-day survival mode to really feeling as if one is living? Being able to breathe without looking over one's shoulder? You have to shift your thinking. After reading each term about society's status levels, I want you to visualize yourself in that position, making that mind shift. What sector of the population would you like to be a part of? For me, it was the part of the population experiencing generational wealth, and I was ready to start building. Yes, it could be seen as just an aspirational goal for some, but I knew it would be much more than that for me. It would eventually be my reality. Like Malcom X famously said, "By any means necessary." Period!

While money is indeed a tool of life, I had to adjust my thinking to realize that it wasn't only something to earn, but, going forward, what I could or would do with my money was what really mattered. See, money only unlocks what's already jailed inside of you. It's how you think. If you are a person who gets money and splurges on material things, you will spend your last dime on "wants" with no care in the world, instead of how you should be using it to better your situation and using money wisely for your needs. Spending money foolishly definitely puts you in the mindset of the working class. This is how you test yourself to find out what type of spender or saver you are: ask yourself how much money did you spent at the store this month. Were they necessary purchases?

In prison, they'd feed you only a certain amount of food at chow time so it would be necessary for you to buy any extra food either, in the commissary or run up a "debt" with your homegirl in the kitchen. The number-one rule on the inside is not to get comfortable but to stay uncomfortable. You must never forget that prisons are a business. They get paid from you being there: your pain, your tears, and your regrets matters not at all to them. Public prisons are owned and operated by state and local government. And ever since the big push for the war on drugs starting in the 1980s, there has been a major increase in inmates in the prison population, causing an ongoing overpopulation.

Public prisons now outsource food, medical care, transportation and vocational training to private companies. These private firms saw an opportunity for a continual increase in their bottom lines (their pockets) and many are now making billions of dollars per year off of these inmates. Two major companies that own and operate private prison in the United States are CCA (Core Civic) and the Geo Group. You learn a lot about Geo, especially once you are put into a halfway house. Private prisons are modeled are to build and manage buildings, secure government contracts and charge a daily fee for each bed filled. Many aspects of prison may still be public, but quite a few public prisons have contracts with these companies. When you run businesses for profit, your main objective will always be to cut costs while increasing revenue. You want to lower your expenses so that you'll be able to take home more money. It's that simple.

How is this any different from the dope game? Just like in the dope game, when you have a good product with high demand the first thing you're going to do is cut the dope so that you spend less money but increase your profit. But to me, to cutting the costs when caring for human beings is unthinkable and often inhumane. You cannot even imagine how deplorable living conditions can be on the inside. I thank God often that I was released just before COVID-19 hit.

Everyday seemed like the day before: waking up, only to slave away for pennies an hour while busting my ass working on the compound. I want you to think about that? Do you really think is it worth giving back what little bit you would earn a day right back into their system or would you prefer to take those measly few cents that you make a day and start investing that amount into *yourself*? This is the same system that was built to break you and make you feel unworthy and as if you can't have a future outside of those prison walls. I'm here to tell you: that's 100 percent bullshit, pure and simple! So instead of using those few pennies to contribute to that seemingly never-ending cycle of failure and doom, do the opposite and use it to invest in yourself.

The most powerful thing you can do while incarcerated is to possess an idea, a vision, a dream for a brighter future once released. So please do not believe the rhetoric they're poisoning you with. Do not believe their politics, the jailhouse "philosophers" or those petty-ass, miserable guards. While it's been said that misery loves company, that does not mean that you have to sit with it or entertain it. Believe in yourself, because you are worth it. You can overcome. You are alive today, whereas someone you possibly know didn't make it through the night. Changing your mindset on your path to building generational wealth starts right here, right now.

Write down your goals. What's at the forefront of your mind? What is your vision for your life? No matter what anyone tells you, if you're willing to work hard, it is attainable. After you write your goals down, I want you to paste them right on your wall so you can work at them every day; keep your vision in front of you. Now it's time to stack more than you spend.

Goal Sheet

- 1
- 2
- 3
- 4
- 5
- 6
- 7
- 8
- 9
- 10
- 11
- 12
- 13
- 14
- 15
- 16
- 17
- 18
- 19
- 20

Chapter Two

MONEY MANAGEMENT

It's time to start stacking more than you spend! Going forward, money management will be is everything to you—how you handle it, as well as, how you deal with it. It's important for you to save while in prison, because you're going to be able to invest what you save right back into yourself. Yes, that's right: you're going to make those little copper pennies work for you. Everything you save is going toward your goals and your dreams. Going forward, you're going to start working everyday on the goals you wrote down earlier for your vision board. Work at them every single day. Your savings will be the capital you invest into yourself. No one is going to do it for you; you'll have to make it happen.

Warren Buffett once told a group of students about a dream he had had when he was a teenager. "Let's say that when I turned sixteen, a genie had appeared to me. And that genie said, 'Warren, I'm going to give you the car of your choice. It'll be here tomorrow morning with a big bow tied on it. Brand-new. And it's all yours.' Having heard all the genie stories, I would say, 'What's the catch?' And the genie would answer, 'There's only one catch. This is the last car you're ever going to get in your life. So it's got to last a lifetime." He'd have to maintain it with the utmost care and attention. And just like with the car of his dream, he went on to say to the young students, "That's exactly the position you are in concerning your mind and body. You only get one mind and one body. And it's got to last a lifetime." But unlike the car situation in Mr. Buffett's dream, in life things are rarely so very black or white; we often *do* get second chances—in our jobs, in our relationships, and in our choices.

And even though I know this to be true, I still keep the thought in the back of my mind that tomorrow is not promised to me, so I need to take advantage of each and every day. Even in my darkest moments, when it has seemed like things couldn't get any worse, I've had to remember that with each new tomorrow, each new sunrise, lies the possibility of a second (new) chance. Always remember that. The greater questions, of course, are these: Will I recognize it? And what will I do with it?

Don't look at your goals and think they are impossible. Look at them and think that they *are* possible—better yet, *I'm* possible. Because whatever you truly set your mind to do, you *can* accomplish it. And you will. Just believe in yourself, even when others doubt you.

As you can imagine, there are very limited resources in prison, educational and otherwise, but is that really any different than the poverty-stricken lifestyle we came from? The few resources that are available to you, books like *"Rich Dad, Poor Dad"* are still floating around in there and are a must-reads for your mental growth. Other resources you must take advantage of are the jobs offered on the compound. You must get the highest-paying job on the compound because you will need as much money as possible to work with. I chose to work for Unicor, which was a call center for GMC; it was the highest-paying job there. They started me off at a grade five, which paid me twenty-three cent an hour, but I could move up all the way to a grade one, which at the time paid $1.15 per hour. I had moved all of the way up to a grade two, at which point I was making ninety-two cents an hour. It gave me one hundred $169 a month to work with. Hard to imagine, right? But, regardless of how much money you earn per month, it really comes down to what you do with it. If you can't budget a $169 a month, how will you ever be able to manage $6,900 or even $69,000? Out of my earnings, I spent about $30 per month: $10 for personal hygiene products, $10 on phone calls and emails and $10 on stamps or certified mail. I had to make my money work for me the best way I could in those circumstances.

Money really is all a game, and you must learn how to play it. The prison system knows how to play the game, profiting off of people very well and winning at it. So are the public schools systems. They really aren't teaching the average person about money and the real world. And if you don't know how to play the game, how are you ever going to win? If you ask me, schools want to keep the working and middle classes right where they're at: in the dark. They don't want us to know what the rich people know. That's how they keep us in a poverty mindset. I feel that our academic system is so corrupt. It doesn't set us up to win but instead to fail.

During the pandemic, schools had to turn to virtual learning. I often sat with my children through their classes and immediately realized how much of a joke, and how damaging, this "new technology" and not being inside an actual classroom was for our children. Studies have shown that it proved especially damaging to children of color. An article published by CNBC (February 23, 2021) quoted Jimmy Sarakatsannis as saying, "Learning loss is happening. It is real and it is inequitable." The article even spoke about how children of color will earn less in their lifetime because of COVD-19. That's why it's important to retain this information, play the game to win, and give right back to the next generation that's coming up behind us. For those of you still in prison, just take a look around you at all the stories you hear or share with one another. How many truly know how to play the game? None! Because if they did, trust me they wouldn't be in there next to you. How many went to a school that taught them about money? If you learn the game now and how to play it and how to apply it to your life and the circumstances you're in right now, you will be breaking that curse. But you must be willing to unlearn everything you've thought about money.

Try going back and playing the game of Monopoly. Start to look at even the play money in a whole new way. Think about how you can double, triple and even quadruple it and how you can get it to work for you by making wise business decisions. Whether you're buying a plastic "hotel" for Park Place or a duplex, it's all the same once you get out. It's all about a mindset shift and making your money work for you. Think about all the money that has come through your hands. What did you do with it? That's why it's important to know who you are with money and how have you operated in the past with it—but more importantly, how you will interact with it going forward. What's your risk tolerance when it comes to money? If you have bad money habits, you can change them today, right now because now you have the tools to change the way you view money.

PAYMENT TO YOURSELF

Money is not the root of all evil the *love* of money is. Do not allow it to consume your thoughts greedily, with desperate thoughts of always having to have it at any cost. You must learn how it works and the true value of money so that once you do start to get it, more and more will come to you. It's the law of attraction: money will flow freely into your life.

You should start by writing yourself a check in the amount you'd like to see in your future and carry that check with you daily.

Visualizing the life you want and what you want in life should become a habit that you embrace and use. Visualization equals manifestation. Always remember that money is just a tool, but how can you best make it work for you? It's a must to make every single penny you earn work for you, no matter your situation. Get a piece of paper. Write down all the income you have coming in monthly: your job on the compound, a side hustle, even money that family and friends may be putting on your books. Write down every penny. Then under that, write down everything you spend. What do you spend at the store? Are you getting your toenails and fingernails painted, your hair cut? Are you getting extra food out of the kitchen? Are you buying extra laundry? Big or small, write it all down.

Now let's talk income versus expenses. The difference between these two is quite simple: income is the money you take in (earn), and expenses are what you spend your money on. Have you heard about the fifty-thirty-twenty (50/30/20) rule in personal finance? That's where 50 percent

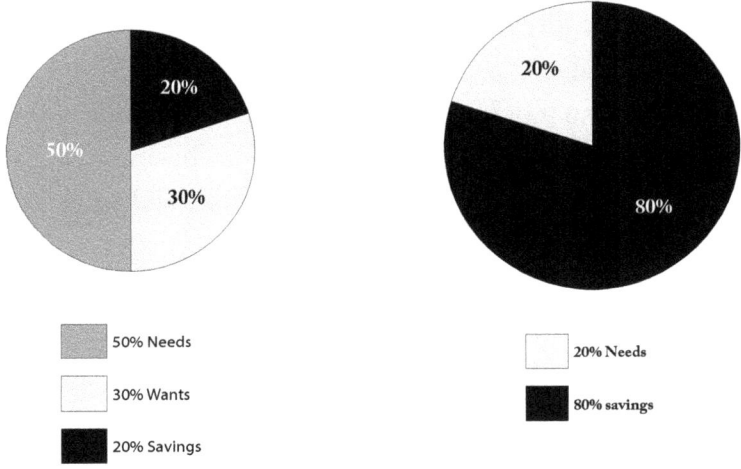

- 50% Needs
- 30% Wants
- 20% Savings

- 20% Needs
- 80% savings

of your money goes towards your needs, 30 percent toward your wants and 20 percent toward savings. Well that rule won't work here. Instead it'll be all about the eighty-twenty (80/20) rule:

Here, 80 percent of your money will go towards your savings and only 20 percent will be set aside for your needs. You will need to write down your goals and make it a habit to look at them daily as a reminder of what you need to accomplish going forward, making sure that your wants (20 percent) never outweigh your needs (80 percent). If you're not noticing this change then that means you're still living in a poverty, day-by-day mindset and you need to fix that fast.

Even if your expenses *don't* outweigh your income, still review your list often to find some things that you can possibly cut back on even further to save even more money. While hygienic products are a must, outside of those items, what more do you really need? This is important if you start getting in the habit of managing your money more properly and using it as a tool and capital to invest in your future. This is the same mindset you'll need to have in business. What you save in there is your capital, your assets, and in reality, your power!

You know upon release that some of you are going to go to a halfway house. Those of you who are going straight home still need to be prepared for your new lives. You will need to have saved as much money as you can, so start to apply that eighty-twenty (80/20) rule as soon as possible. Capital and a good name (and when I say, "Good name," I'm talking about your credit) will be all you have working for you when starting your new life. You work on and fix your credit right now, while still on the inside. Credit is another very important asset that you'll need to have work for you. Good credit can provide you with more capital to invest in your future and in yourself. You just have to apply it right and leverage it in the right way. This is one of the reasons why you have been saving. You're going to start using some of that capital to get your credit right long before you walk out those doors.

Chapter Three

CHECK MY CREDIT; MY NAME'S GOOD

CREDIT IS OFFERED TO A CONSUMER TO OBTAIN GOODS or services before any payment is given based on the trust that the payment will be paid back at a future date. When you think about credit think about it in a true hustler's form. So if you run a store in there and someone gets something from you, the only thing they have to bargain with is their word. You give them a set date to pay you back (with interest) and if they do pay you back *and* on time, they are considered in good standing with you. Thus, when they come back and want to borrow something of an even greater amount/value, you're willing to do so because they made good on the last exchange; they're showing their creditworthiness. That's how credit works.

First thing first: Put in a DAR to see your counselor to let them know you are trying to get a copy of your credit report and that you need authorized personnel to verify the prison as your place of residence. You can also use your sentence computation but make sure it's the full print out with your facility and address on it. If not, put the Dar in. Write a request for your credit report. This letter should include your full name (including your middle name), previous mailing address, date of birth, and Social Security number. It should also, as previously mentioned, include the verification of the prison as being your address. Send this letter out to all three major credit bureaus: TransUnion, Equifax and Experian. Every year, you are entitled to a free credit report from each one of these credit-reporting agencies. And you definitely want to take advantage of receiving a report from all three of them to verify all pertinent information since not every account is reported to all three agencies.

The Fair Credit Reporting Act (FCRA), with fiften USC sections (1681—1681t), protects you against credit abuse that might result in unfair descriptions of your creditworthiness. Knowing your six basic rights is essential if you are going to erase negative marks off of your credit report and regain good credit status:

- **Right 1**: You are allowed to challenge the accuracy of your credit report at any time.
- **Right 2**: The credit bureau(s) must investigate, in good faith, anything that you challenge.
- **Right 3**: The credit bureau(s) must re-investigate the disputed information within thirty days (as a matter

of law). There are exceptions to the time period if the bureau requests additional information.
- **Right 4**: If the credit bureau cannot confirm the adverse information or finds any errors, it must promptly delete that erroneous information from its files.
- **Right 5**: If the bureau cannot or does not confirm the information you have challenged within a reasonable amount of time, it must also delete that information from your files.
- **Right 6**: If a creditor verifies the information and the bureau responds promptly, the negative marks must remain on your record. But if you maintain that the information reported is in dispute, you have the right to submit a "customer statement" of your view of the problem. If you, as the credit consumer, dispute the accuracy of certain information on your report and receive no satisfaction from the bureau or the creditor, then the credit bureau is by law required to attach your explanation to every copy of the report it sends out. If you ask for assistance the bureau will help you write your statement of one hundred words.

Should you choose to dispute information on one, or all of your reports, here are the addresses of each Credit Reporting Agencies, as well as, an example of the letter you can write to them:

TransUnion
Post Office Box 1000
Chester, Pennsyklvania 19022

Equifax
Post Office Box 740241
Atlanta, Georgia 30374-0241

Experian
Post Office Box 2104
Allen, Texas 75013-0949

SAMPLE LETTER

Full name: Jane Elizabeth Doe
Social Security number: 123-45-6789
Date of birth: January 1, 2000
Previous address: 421 Johnson Street, Richmond, California 12345

To Whom It May Concern,
I'm requesting a copy of my free credit report. My current mailing address is:

FCI Dublin 5701
8th Floor Street
Dublin, CA 94568

Attached is proof of my residency.
Thank you,

Signature

Once you receive copies of your credit reports, you'll need to review and cross-check every single account for any possible inaccuracy. If any of the accounts show inaccurate information regarding debts, you'll want to dispute it as soon as possible. Your dispute letters don't have to be fancy;

write in plain, simple English, because no one actually reads them. All letters are scanned into a system and a computer filters them into two codes that deciphers keywords and key phrases from your letter(s). Again, be sure to keep your correspondence simple.

Once received, your letter(s) are sent out to a third party company, which will match all your info and try to verify accounts as being yours. One such third party is e-Oscar. They are basically a computer accounting system that holds everyone's personal data like the white pages. The primary job of e-Oscar is to validate your account and verify you as the account holder. They don't need the original signed application; they just want to link that account to you. This company will verify the account link to one of your previous addresses, thus enabling them to verify that the right accounts belongs to you. Before you dispute anything, you will want to look at the personal information on your report and get rid of as much of it as possible, including any old or outdated information such as addresses, phone numbers and even old jobs. There should be only one address being reported on your report.

Your name should be listed only one way; there should be no different variations of it. You should do this before disputing the account is because the third party performing this service is only trying to verify the account as belonging to you. So if the account's listed to a previous address, and that address is reported on your credit report, it will be verified. And if that previous address is not associated with you, then that account may very well be able to qualify for removal. Thus e-Oscar collects data from the following companies: Lexis Nexis, Innovis, Sage Stream, and ARS. Normally, if you had access to a computer, you would go to each of the following websites to freeze your information. But, since you probably won't have access to a computer while still on the inside or two forms of identification, there is another way that you can contact them. You can use the following sample letter format to be in touch with them.

www.LexisNexis.com
www.Innovis.com
www.sagestreamllc.com
www.ars-consumeroffice.com

SAMPLE LETTER

Full name: Jane Elizabeth Doe
Date of birth: January 1, 1945
Social Security number: 123-45-6789
Current address: 421 Johnson Street, Richmond, CA 12345

To Whom It May Concern,
This letter is to correct the spelling of my name. Above is my current address. Please remove all other items from my personal history because I am afraid that I might be susceptible to identity theft.

Signature

    Now is your time to start working on your disputes. Once you receive all three credit reports back, you're going to look at each account and if you notice any inaccurate information being reported, you will dispute it. Even if you are delinquent on any of your accounts, you're still going to dispute it to move forward. On your delinquent accounts you're going to write them a letter explaining that you're incarcerated and that you will not be able to pay the full amount, but you are willing to come to a settlement. Ask what options for repayment they can provide you to settle the account and have it shown as paid. More than likely, you'll be asked to payoff your owed balance in full, or they may even offer terms for a repayment plan. Keep in mind that rarely does anyone payoff a settlement in full; negotiate with them. If you are already delinquent, especially if your account has been turned over to a collection agency, they will be glad to get whatever you're able to pay.

If you end up setting up a payment plan, so just be honest about how much you'll be able to afford to payout each month. This is one of the reasons you have you been saving because you will have to have some money to fight these types of battles. It is so important that everything you mail off is done via certified mail, so that you'll have proof of all correspondence. Disputing inaccurate information can be time consuming and exhausting. But don't get discouraged. Some agencies may challenge you (that's their job), but all you have to do is hit them back with a second dispute letter. It's important to clear all debt before you start building your financial and creditworthy future. If you have no debt that's great: that means you're already putting yourself in a position to start building. Remember that debt can remain on your credit from seven years to ten years. Thus should you see any debt being reported on your credit that's older than seven years (and is not a judgment, an unpaid tax lien, or a chapter 7 bankruptcy), you can have it removed. If you have been the victim of identity theft, any erroneous information related to that will also be removed.

The confidentiality of your medical records is protected by federal health insurance act known as HIPAA, and the

HIPAA law protects you as an individual. You need to remember that those are *your* medical records with *your* personal health information. When a medical facility sells your medical records to a third-party collection agency in order to get help in collecting a debt from you, that is a complete violation of the HIPAA law. Dispute it, but keep in mind that the FCRA does not allow the deletion of debt, even one reported in the case of a HIPAA violation. So you may have to contact the creditor yourself and threaten to sue them for violating the law.

DISPUTE LETTER SAMPLE: DELINQUENT ACCOUNTS

Date:
Full name:
Social Security number:
Date of birth:
Current Address:
Re: Account number 1234-5678-8765-4321

To Whom It May Concern,
Please be aware that this is not an acknowledgment or acceptance of the debt, as I have not received any verification of the debt. Nor is this a promise to pay and is not a payment agreement unless you provide a response as detailed below.

I am currently incarcerated and am willing to pay **[this debt in full / $XXX as settlement for this debt]** in return for your agreement to remove all information regarding this debt from the credit-reporting agencies within ten calendar days of payment. If you agree to the terms, I will send my payment via certified mail, in the amount of **$XXX**. In exchange for doing this, please have all information related to this debt, removed from all my credit files.

If you accept this offer, you also agree not to discuss the offer with any third-party, excluding the original creditor. If you accept the offer, please prepare a letter on your company letterhead agreeing to these terms. This letter should be signed by an authorized agent of (name of collection agency). The letter will be treated as a contract and subject to the laws of my state.

As granted by the Fair Debt Collection Practices Act, I have the right to dispute this alleged debt. If I do not receive your postmarked response within fifteen (15) days, I will withdraw the offer and request full verification of this debt.

Please forward your agreement to the address listed above.

Sincerely,

_____

Your Name

DISPUTE LETTER SAMPLE: IDENTITY THEFT

Full name:
Date of birth:
Social Security number:
Current address:

To Whom It May Concern,
I did not make or authorize these following transactions: (name of debt collector / account number). I am a victim of identity theft and I have enclosed a copy of my credit report that lists the unauthorized accounts. Please remove these accounts from my credit report immediately and send confirmation, to the address shown above, that you have done so.

Sincerely,

_____   _____
Signature   Date

DISPUTE LETTER SAMPLE: MEDICAL

Full name:
Date of birth:
Social Security number:
Current address:

Dear Debt Collection Agent,
I received a bill from you on [date] and as allowed under the Fair Debt Collection Practices Act (FDCPA), I am requesting that you allow me to validate the alleged debt. I am aware that there is a debt from [name of hospital/doctor], but I am unaware of the amount due and your bill does not include a breakdown of any fees.

Additionally, I am allowed under the Health Insurance Portability and Accountability Act (HIPAA) to protect my privacy and medical records from third parties. I do not recall giving permission to [name of provider] for them to release my medical information to a third party. I am aware that the HIPAA does allow for limited information about me but anything more is to only be revealed with the patient's authorization. Therefore my request is twofold—validation of debt and HIPAA authorization.

Please provide breakdown of fees, including any collection costs and medical charges. Provide a copy of my signature with the provider of service to release my medical information to you. Cease any credit bureau reporting until the debt has been validated by me.

Please send this information to my address listed above and accept this letter, sent certified mail, as my formal debt validation request, which I am allowed under the FDCPA. Please note that withholding the information you received from any medical provider in an attempt to be HIPAA compliant can be a violation of the FDCPA because you will be deceiving me after my written request. I request full documentation of what you received from the service provider in connection with this alleged debt. Additionally, any reporting of this debt to the credit bureaus prior to allowing me to validate it may be a violation of the Fair Credit Reporting Act, which can allow me to seek damages from a collection agent. I will await your reply with above-requested proof. Upon receiving it, I will correspond back by certified mail.

Sincerely,

_____   _____
Signature   Date

Chapter Four

ROME WASN'T BUILT IN A DAY

TIME TO START BUILDING. NOT ONLY WILL YOU BE establishing your credit, but you'll also be building the foundation for your future life and your dreams. You should always be working toward your goals. Daily! What's the old saying? "Shoot for the moon and even if you miss, at least you'll be among the stars." Always remember that. As you know, life isn't easy by any means, but the difference between people is that when some of us get knocked down we get right back up…fighting!

Let's talk about trade lines. A primary trade line is a credit account that is opened in your own name, in which the creditor extends credit to you, the borrower. When you open a credit card on your own, you'll then have a primary trade line. This means that you are responsible for all the transactions that occur on that trade line. How do you obtain a primary trade line? Well, you start with a secured credit card. Secured credit cards can be a good option for building or rebuilding your credit, allowing you to establish or reestablish your credit. Since payment histories are included in your credit report, paying on time and managing your balance will help improve your credit score. A secured credit card is backed by a cash deposit you make when you open the account. The deposit is usually equal to your credit limit, so if you were to deposit $200 in an account, then you'd have a $200 spending limit. Your deposit reduces the risk to the credit card issuer. Should you not pay your bill, the issuer can take the money owed from what you have placed on deposit.

The one thing a secured credit card generally won't give you is the ability to actually borrow money, since, in essence, you are only being allowed to use an amount that equals the amount you have at the bank securing your card. If you were to have a credit limit that far exceeded your balance on deposit at your bank then you'd have a regular (un-secured) credit card. And repayments on balances racked up with an unsecured card aren't guaranteed, so issuers often charge high interest rates and non-refundable fees to mitigate their risk.

The combination of high approval rates and low fees make secured cards the best tool available for building or rebuilding your credit. But they're still fairly unfamiliar to most people. So I'll give you a step-by-step overview of what to expect when you get one.

Here's how a Secured Credit Card works. You place a refundable security deposit using a bank transfer. A debit card or check could be an option, too, depending on the card. Some secured cards require you to place a deposit when you apply, others do so after you're approved. The minimum deposit for most secured cards is $200 or $300.

The amount of your deposit becomes your spending limit. This prevents you from spending more than you can afford to repay, which benefits both you and the card issuer in the long run. For what it's worth, you can usually add to your deposit over time for more spending power. The credit card company holds your deposit as collateral. The funds are usually kept in a custodial account that does not bear interest.

Purchases and payments are the same as with any other credit card. You can spend up to your credit limit. You'll have to pay your bill by the due date each month. And any balance you carry from month to month will accrue interest.

You get the deposit back when you close your account. You'll have to bring your account balance to zero first. But after you do (or the issuer subtracts what you owe), you'll get a check or bank transfer returning your remaining deposited money.

After using a secured credit card responsibly for at least twelve (12) months, you should be able to graduate to an unsecured credit card. Your secured card's issuer might even offer to convert your account to unsecured by giving back your security deposit. If your card doesn't charge an annual fee, you should definitely consider keeping it open. This would help make your credit history appear longer, benefitting your credit score. But you should still shop around to see if you qualify for a better card to use on an everyday basis.

You can track your progress for free on WalletHub, the only site with free credit scores and reports that are updated daily. You'll also receive personalized credit- improvement advice to help you graduate to an unsecured card sooner.

Here are a few places that you can try for your card:

- OpenSky Secured Visa Credit Card
- First National Bank of Omaha Secured Visa Card
- Citi Secured Mastercard
- Discover It Secured Card (Build Your Credit History) https://www.discover.com/
- Chime Credit Builder Card (No Credit Check to Apply) https://www.chime.com/ Chime is fairly new but what's unique about getting a Chime account it operates very much like a bank account. So I suggest that even while you're still in prison, try to reach out to reach out to someone you trust and ask them to open you a Chime account. Chime offers secured cards, as well.

Are you familiar with the term "authorized user?" An authorized user is an additional cardholder on someone else's credit card account. Becoming an authorized user on a credit card, gas card or store card is one way to improve your credit history without having to be on the hook for monthly payments. Authorized users don't have the same abilities as a primary cardholder, like requesting an increase in the credit line, but adding an authorized user can be beneficial to both the primary cardholder and the authorized user. The primary cardholder can enlist an authorized user to help meet spending requirements. Meanwhile, the authorized user can establish a credit history.

That's one of the great benefits of piggybacking off of someone else's credit card. You'll be able to build your own credit history and, by doing so, establish your own credit report. Basically, your credit history is important because lenders, insurers, employers, and others may use it to assess how you manage financial responsibilities. History is everything so stay consistent in establishing a great credit history. No more being late or delinquent on your accounts. Remember, if you have someone you can reach out to who can add you as an authorized user on their account, please do so. If not, I have resources you can utilize to get started. Just email an agent at Americanfederaltaxco@gmail.com and they'll be able to help you get started in establishing your credit. Good luck!

Chapter Five

LEVERAGE MORE THAN WHAT'S BETWEEN YOUR LEGS

JUST IN CASE YOU HAVEN'T COME TO REALIZED IT YET, AT the end of the day, you and only you, are responsible for your future. No matter how wonderful it may sound, Superman is not coming to save you. Period! If you have any thoughts of getting a man to take care of you, please let them go. How many of you are sitting behind bars right now, or recently have been, because of a man? A man that you chose to follow, to love, to be loyal to and dedicated to? How many of you are broken because he left you (and your children) and fed you to the wolves to save his own skin? That was definitely me.

I was broken because I'd placed a man above myself for over twelve years. Thinking back, I knew the entire time I was dancing with the devil. I knew who he was because he showed me time and time again, but I chose to see nothing but the good in him, believing that if I loved him just a little bit harder and rode for him just a little longer, I could change him. Over time, I thought that things would work out. But in bad situations, rarely is time on our side. And by being that "ride or die" chick for him, I had lost the real essence of myself along the way. And when the pressure was applied to him, sure enough, he didn't stand solidly for me at all!

I know many of you can relate. Just look out at the visiting rooms in a women's prison—not packed at all. Even Clyde rode with Bonnie till the very end. But trust and believe that scenario is very rare. It doesn't seem fair because, as women, when choosing a man we often are looking for the three P's: partner, protector and provider. But in reality, we are often left with a punk. You want to feel safe. You want to feel that it's you and that person against the world—someone to love the pain away, someone to face all your demons and your trials and tribulations with, someone to ride with you to the very end. Do not harbor that pain. Let it go! Your journey to healing, your life, your soul—and yes, your finances—starts today.

When you have negative thoughts about that person, about that man who left you hanging, then you are keeping the negativity alive in your own spirit and are allowing it to continually come back to you. So put the past exactly where it belongs: in the past! All previous notions about who you thought someone else was or was going to be for you are over. Time to own up to your choices and take accountability for why you have allowed people—a man, a woman, a friend or a relative—to manipulate, misguide and abuse you. To truly come to terms with where your life is currently at, you must sit and dwell in every emotion that you have, both the positives and the negatives. You must really own, acknowledge and understand them to get to their cores, embrace the positive and break away from the negative. It's time to start embracing a new you; starting here, starting now. Now is your time to become whole again, or maybe whole for the first time! When you release those people from your thoughts, you begin to understand who you are and gain your power back.

When you're broken it's one thing to shift your mindset, but in order to become completely committed, not only do when need to change the way we think, but we also need to change how we process our feelings. You must clean up what's inside of you. If you fill a dirty glass with clean water, not only is the glass still dirty, but now the water that you need for survival is also dirty. So you must start with a clean vessel (yourself). Before adding anything to it, ask yourself, "Is who or what I'm going to allow inside my body and soul also clean and beneficial, or is it dirty and toxic?"

Next to your vision board where you earlier wrote down your goals and dreams, I want you to also write down the woman you want to become. Write down her physical appearance: how she looks, her hairstyle, the way she dresses, the way she smells. Write down everything to the smallest detail, even her hygiene. Do not leave anything about her out. Write it all down. Write down her mindset, the way you'd like for her to think and act. Write down the way she operates. Then write about her spirit; how she feels, how she loves, and, equally important, how she *wants* to be loved. Write down how she is as a mother, a sister, a daughter, a friend. Write down how you envision her as a lover and confidante. Write down what type of man she's going to allow in her life going forward. Write down what type of man she'd like to marry and be her life partner. Write down the type of car that you see her driving and the style of home that she'll live in. Write down the types of businesses you'd like for her to own.

Today, you are snatching back your power, only making positive moves from this moment on. It was important for me to do this to know who I was/ and who I am as a person. What are my capabilities? I just needed to let go of all the excuses and negative thoughts and environments that were, in actuality, holding me back. In those last ten months of my unfortunate incarceration, my mindset had truly shifted and I was ready to win. I had everything to gain and nothing to lose. I believe the same is also true for you.

One of the greatest things you can possess is knowing who you are presently as a person and who you desire to be. Don't listen to what the guards, your cell mate, society or even the judge says about you. Believe me, at the end of the day, it's what you say about yourself that matters. It's not going to be easy, for change never is, but you already know what struggle and adversity look like. So what more do you have to lose? You've been to the bottom, now it's time to rise to the top. Do *not* let anyone or anything deter you from being the queen that you are meant to be—not your past, your surroundings, you circumstances, or your upbringing. Do not let anything stand in your way. Greatness is a part of you. It's just on the other side of that wall waiting for you to go and get it. You got this!

Carpe Diem,
Stasha

NOTES:

www.ingramcontent.com/pod-product-compliance
Ingram Content Group UK Ltd.
Pitfield, Milton Keynes, MK11 3LW, UK
UKHW022237230426
12048UKWH00018BA/1318